FAVORITE BRAND NAME™

Classroom Treats

Publications International, Ltd.
Favorite Brand Name Recipes at www.fbnr.com

Pictured on the front cover: Glazed Donut Cookies *(page 112).*
Pictured on the back cover *(left to right):* Brontosaurus Bites *(page 14)* and Rainbow Spirals *(page 106).*

Microwave Cooking: Microwave ovens vary in wattage. Use the cooking times as guidelines and check for doneness before adding more time.

Preparation/Cooking Times: Preparation times are based on the approximate amount of time required to assemble the recipe before cooking, baking, chilling or serving. These times include preparation steps such as measuring, chopping and mixing. The fact that some preparations and cooking can be done simultaneously is taken into account. Preparation of optional ingredients and serving suggestions is not included.

Contents

Crunchy Snack Mixes

Find endless combinations for snack mixes that kids are sure to love. Fill decorated goodie bags or party cups for easy-to-serve crunchy treats.

Spicy, Fruity Popcorn Mix

- 4 cups lightly salted popcorn
- 2 cups corn cereal squares
- 1½ cups dried pineapple wedges
- 1 package (6 ounces) dried fruit bits
  Butter-flavored nonstick cooking spray
- 2 tablespoons sugar
- 1 tablespoon ground cinnamon
- 1 cup yogurt-covered raisins

1. Preheat oven to 350°F. Combine popcorn, cereal, pineapple and fruit bits in large bowl; mix lightly. Transfer to 15×10-inch jelly-roll pan. Spray mixture generously with cooking spray.

2. Combine sugar and cinnamon in small bowl. Sprinkle ½ of the sugar mixture over popcorn mixture; toss lightly to coat. Spray mixture again with additional cooking spray. Add remaining sugar mixture; mix lightly.

3. Bake snack mix 10 minutes, stirring after 5 minutes. Cool completely in pan on wire rack. Add raisins; mix lightly. *Makes 7 to 8 cups*

Spicy, Fruity Popcorn Mix ✳ 7

Cinnamon Trail Mix

    2 cups corn cereal squares
    2 cups whole wheat cereal squares or whole wheat
        cereal squares with mini graham crackers
1½ cups fat-free oyster crackers
    ½ cup broken sesame snack sticks
    2 tablespoons margarine or butter, melted
    1 teaspoon ground cinnamon
    ¼ teaspoon ground nutmeg
    ½ cup bite-size fruit-flavored candy pieces

1. Preheat oven to 350°F. Spray 13×9-inch baking pan with nonstick cooking spray.

2. Place cereals, oyster crackers and sesame sticks in prepared pan; mix lightly.

3. Combine margarine, cinnamon and nutmeg in small bowl; mix well. Drizzle evenly over cereal mixture; toss to coat.

4. Bake 12 to 14 minutes or until golden brown, stirring gently after 6 minutes. Cool completely. Stir in candies.   *Makes 6 cups*

Critter Munch

1½ cups animal cracker cookies
    ½ (6-ounce) package cheddar or original flavor
        goldfish crackers (1½ cups)
    1 cup dried tart cherries
    1 cup candy-coated chocolate candy
    1 cup honey roasted peanuts (optional)

1. Put animal crackers, goldfish crackers, dried cherries, candy and peanuts, if desired, in a large mixing bowl.

2. Carefully stir with a spoon.

3. Store in a tightly covered container at room temperature.
                                                    Makes 5 cups

Favorite recipe from **Cherry Marketing Institute**

Cinnamon Trail Mix ✗ 9

Popcorn Crunchies

- **12 cups popped corn (about ¾ cup unpopped)**
- **1½ cups sugar**
- **⅓ cup water**
- **⅓ cup corn syrup**
- **2 tablespoons butter or margarine**
- **1 teaspoon vanilla**

1. Preheat oven to 250°F. Grease large shallow roasting pan. Add popcorn. Keep warm in oven while making caramel mixture.

2. Place sugar, water and corn syrup in heavy 2-quart saucepan. Stir over low heat until sugar has dissolved and mixture comes to a boil. Carefully clip candy thermometer to side of pan (do not let bulb touch bottom of pan). Cook over low heat, without stirring, about 10 minutes or until thermometer registers 280°F. Occasionally wash down any sugar crystals that form on side of the pan using pastry brush dipped in warm water. Immediately remove from heat. Stir in butter and vanilla until smooth.

3. Pour hot syrup mixture slowly over warm popcorn, turning to coat kernels evenly. Set aside until cool enough to handle but warm enough to shape. Butter hands. Working quickly, lightly press warm mixture into 2-inch balls. Cool completely. Store in airtight container.

Makes about 14 popcorn balls

Make It Special

Popcorn Crunchies also make fabulous tree ornaments. Cool balls completely and wrap each ball with enough decorative plastic wrap to pull wrap together at the top. Secure with a ribbon which can be formed into a bow or a loop for hanging.

Pleasin' Peanutty Snack Mix

4 cups whole wheat cereal squares *or* 2 cups whole wheat and
    2 cups corn or rice cereal squares
2 cups small pretzel twists or goldfish-shaped pretzels
½ cup dry-roasted peanuts
2 tablespoons creamy peanut butter
1 tablespoon honey
1 tablespoon apple juice or water
2 teaspoons vanilla
    Butter-flavored nonstick cooking spray
½ cup raisins, dried fruit bits or dried cherries (optional)

1. Preheat oven to 250°F.

2. Combine cereal, pretzels and peanuts in large bowl; set aside.

3. Combine peanut butter, honey and apple juice in small microwavable bowl. Microwave at HIGH 30 seconds or until hot. Stir in vanilla.

4. Drizzle peanut butter mixture evenly over cereal mixture; toss lightly to evenly coat. Place mixture in single layer in ungreased 15×10-inch jelly-roll pan; coat lightly with cooking spray.

5. Bake 8 minutes; stir. Continue baking 8 to 9 minutes or until golden brown. Remove from oven. Add raisins, if desired; mix lightly.

6. Spread mixture in single layer on large sheet of foil to cool.

Makes 6 cups

 Make It Special

Add excitement to the party by using empty ice cream cones as individual edible serving bowls for serving snack mixes. Look for colored cones to add extra pizzazz.

Brontosaurus Bites

    4 cups air-popped popcorn
    2 cups mini-dinosaur grahams
    2 cups corn cereal squares
 1½ cups dried pineapple wedges
    1 package (6 ounces) dried fruit bits
      Butter-flavored nonstick cooking spray
    1 tablespoon plus 1½ teaspoons sugar
 1½ teaspoons ground cinnamon
   ½ teaspoon ground nutmeg
    1 cup yogurt-covered raisins

1. Preheat oven to 350°F. Combine popcorn, grahams, cereal, pineapple and fruit bits in large bowl; mix lightly. Transfer to 15×10-inch jelly-roll pan. Spray mixture generously with cooking spray.

2. Combine sugar, cinnamon and nutmeg in small bowl. Sprinkle ½ of the sugar mixture over popcorn mixture; toss lightly to coat. Spray mixture again with additional cooking spray. Add remaining sugar mixture; mix lightly.

3. Bake snack mix 10 minutes, stirring after 5 minutes. Cool completely in pan on wire rack. Add raisins; mix lightly.   *Makes about 9 cups*

Gorilla Grub: Substitute plain raisins for the yogurt-covered raisins and ¼ cup grated Parmesan cheese for the sugar, cinnamon and nutmeg.

Make It Special

Kids may want to bring snacks home. Pick up small sturdy paper plates, clear plastic bags and assorted colorful ribbons. Or, prepare take-home treats ahead of time. Wrap extra snack mix in festive colored paper napkins, party bags or small plastic food storage bags decorated with stickers.

Sticks 'n' Stones

  4 cups caramel corn
  4 cups unseasoned croutons
  ¾ cup sesame sticks
  ¾ cup honey roasted peanuts (optional)
  ¾ cup toasted pumpkin or sunflower seeds*
  ¼ cup (½ stick) butter, melted
  1 package (1 ounce) dry ranch-style salad dressing mix
 10 flat-bottomed ice cream cones

To toast seeds, place in single layer on baking sheet. Bake at 350°F for 7 to 10 minutes or until golden brown, stirring occasionally. Cool completely.

1. Preheat oven to 300°F.

2. Combine caramel corn, croutons, sesame sticks, peanuts, if desired, and toasted pumpkin seeds on ungreased jelly-roll pan. Drizzle with butter; sprinkle with dressing mix and toss to coat.

3. Bake 15 minutes, stirring occasionally. Cool 10 minutes on pan. Turn out onto paper towels; cool completely.

4. Tie cones with ribbons, if desired. Serve snack mix in cones.

Makes 10 cups

Original Ranch® Snack Mix

  8 cups KELLOGG'S® CRISPIX®** cereal
 2½ cups small pretzels
 2½ cups bite-size Cheddar cheese crackers (optional)
  3 tablespoons vegetable oil
  1 packet (1 ounce) HIDDEN VALLEY® The Original Ranch®
    Salad Dressing & Seasoning Mix

Kellogg's® and Crispix® are registered trademarks of Kellogg Company.

Combine cereal, pretzels and crackers in a gallon-size Glad® Zipper Storage Bag. Pour oil over mixture. Seal bag and toss to coat. Add salad dressing & seasoning mix; seal bag and toss again until coated.

Makes 10 cups

Chocolate & Fruit Snack Mix

½ cup (1 stick) butter or margarine
2 tablespoons sugar
1 tablespoon HERSHEY'S Cocoa or
   HERSHEY'S Dutch Processed Cocoa
½ teaspoon ground cinnamon
3 cups bite-size crisp rice squares cereal
3 cups bite-size crisp wheat squares cereal
2 cups toasted oat cereal rings
1 cup cashews
1½ cups (6-ounce package) dried fruit bits
1 cup HERSHEY'S Semi-Sweet Chocolate Chips

1. Place butter in 4-quart microwave-safe bowl. Microwave at HIGH (100%) 1 minute or until melted; stir in sugar, cocoa and cinnamon. Add cereals and cashews; stir until evenly coated. Microwave at HIGH 3 minutes, stirring after each minute; stir in dried fruit. Microwave at HIGH 3 minutes, stirring after each minute.

2. Cool completely; stir in chocolate chips. Store in tightly covered container in cool, dry place.   *Makes about 11 cups*

Patchwork Pop Corn Party Mix

3 quarts popped JOLLY TIME® Pop Corn
2 cups rice or wheat cereal squares
½ cup dried cranberries or dried tart cherries
1 cup coarsely chopped walnuts, toasted
3 tablespoons butter or margarine
½ teaspoon maple extract

Place popped pop corn, cereal, cranberries and walnuts in large bowl. Melt butter in small pan. Stir in maple extract. Pour over pop corn mixture; toss well.   *Makes about 14 cups*

Holiday Party Mix

    9 cups oven-toasted corn cereal squares
    4 cups popped popcorn
1½ cups dry-roasted peanuts
    1 cup packed light brown sugar
    ½ cup (1 stick) butter or margarine
    ½ cup light corn syrup
    1 teaspoon vanilla extract
    ½ teaspoon baking soda
1¾ cups (10-ounce package) NESTLÉ® TOLL HOUSE® Holiday
        Shapes & Morsels
    1 package (7.5 ounces) white fudge-covered pretzels

PREHEAT oven to 250°F. Grease large roasting pan.

MIX cereal, popped popcorn and peanuts in large bowl. Pour into prepared pan.

COMBINE brown sugar, butter and corn syrup in medium, *heavy-duty* saucepan. Bring to a boil over medium heat, stirring constantly. Boil, without stirring, for 5 minutes. Remove from heat; stir in vanilla extract and baking soda. Pour evenly over cereal mixture; stir to coat evenly.

BAKE for 45 minutes, stirring every 15 minutes. Cool completely in pan, stirring frequently to break apart mixture. Stir in Shapes & Morsels and pretzels. Store in airtight container.   *Makes about 20 cups*

Make It Special

Be sure to take advantage of seasonally decorated, shaped or colored food items like morsels and pretzels. These special holiday items make it easy to add that extra touch to holiday treats.

Teddy Bear Party Mix

4 cups crisp cinnamon graham cereal
2 cups honey flavored teddy-shaped graham snacks
1 can (1½ ounces) *French's*® Potato Sticks
3 tablespoons melted unsalted butter
2 tablespoons *French's*® Worcestershire Sauce
1 tablespoon packed brown sugar
¼ teaspoon ground cinnamon
1 cup sweetened dried cranberries or raisins
½ cup chocolate, peanut butter or carob chips

1. Preheat oven to 350°F. Lightly spray jelly-roll pan with nonstick cooking spray. Combine cereal, graham snacks and potato sticks in large bowl.

2. Combine butter, Worcestershire, sugar and cinnamon in small bowl; toss with cereal mixture. Transfer to prepared pan. Bake 12 minutes. Cool completely.

3. Stir in dried cranberries and chips. Store in an air-tight container.

Makes about 7 cups

Prep Time: 5 minutes • Cook Time: 12 minutes

Cereal Trail Mix

¼ cup (½ stick) butter or margarine
2 tablespoons sugar
1 teaspoon ground cinnamon
1 cup bite-size oat cereal squares
1 cup bite-size wheat cereal squares
1 cup bite-size rice cereal squares
¼ cup toasted slivered almonds
¾ cup raisins

Melt butter at HIGH 1½ minutes in large microwave-safe bowl. Add sugar and cinnamon; mix well. Add cereals and nuts; stir to coat. Microwave at HIGH 2 minutes. Stir well. Microwave 2 minutes more; stir well. Add raisins. Microwave an additional 2 to 3 minutes, stirring well after 2 minutes. Spread on paper towels; mix will become crisp as it cools. Store tightly covered.

Makes about 4 cups

Birthday Parties

Make birthdays extra special with attractively decorated treats.
Colorful homemade cookies, cakes or cupcakes
make any party memorable.

Dipped, Drizzled & Decorated Pretzels

1 bag chocolate or flavored chips (choose semisweet, bittersweet, milk chocolate, green mint, white chocolate, butterscotch, peanut butter or a combination)
1 bag pretzel rods
   Assorted toppings: jimmies, sprinkles, chopped nuts, coconut, toasted coconut, cookie crumbs, colored sugars

Microwave Directions

1. Place chips in microwavable bowl. (Be sure bowl and utensils are completely dry.) Cover with plastic wrap and turn back one corner to vent. Microwave at HIGH for 1 minute; stir. Return to microwave and continue cooking in 30-second intervals until chips are completely melted. Check and stir frequently.

2. Dip one half of each pretzel rod into melted chocolate and decorate. Roll coated end of several pretzels in toppings. Drizzle others with contrasting color/flavor melted chips. (Drizzle melted chocolate out of spoon while rotating pretzel, to get even coverage.)

3. Place decorated pretzels on cooling rack; set over baking sheet lined with waxed-paper. Let coating harden completely. Do not refrigerate.

Makes about 24 pretzels

Cookies & Cream Cupcakes

2¼ cups all-purpose flour
1 tablespoon baking powder
½ teaspoon salt
1⅔ cups sugar
1 cup milk
½ cup (1 stick) butter, softened
2 teaspoons vanilla
3 egg whites
1 cup crushed chocolate sandwich cookies (about 10 cookies) plus additional for garnish
1 container (16 ounces) vanilla frosting

1. Preheat oven to 350°F. Line 24 regular-size (2½-inch) muffin pan cups with paper baking cups.

2. Sift flour, baking powder and salt together in large bowl. Stir in sugar. Add milk, butter and vanilla; beat with electric mixer at low speed 30 seconds. Beat at medium speed 2 minutes. Add egg whites; beat 2 minutes. Stir in 1 cup crushed cookies.

3. Spoon batter into prepared muffin cups. Bake 20 to 25 minutes or until toothpicks inserted into centers come out clean. Cool in pans on wire racks 10 minutes. Remove to racks; cool completely.

4. Frost cupcakes; garnish with additional crushed cookies.

Makes 24 cupcakes

Make It Special

Tempt small appetites with miniature-size instead of regular-size cupcakes. Children and moms will enjoy these bite-size goodies that are tasty, colorful, fun and less messy to eat.

Banana Split Cupcakes

    1 package (about 18 ounces) yellow cake mix, divided
    1 cup water
    1 cup mashed ripe bananas
    3 eggs
    1 cup chopped drained maraschino cherries
 1½ cups miniature semisweet chocolate chips, divided
 1½ cups prepared vanilla frosting
    1 cup marshmallow creme
    1 teaspoon shortening
  30 whole maraschino cherries, drained and patted dry

1. Preheat oven to 350°F. Line 30 regular-size (2½-inch) muffin cups with paper baking cups.

2. Reserve 2 tablespoons cake mix. Combine remaining cake mix, water, bananas and eggs in large bowl. Beat at low speed of electric mixer until moistened, about 30 seconds. Beat at medium speed 2 minutes. Combine chopped cherries and reserved cake mix in small bowl. Stir chopped cherry mixture and 1 cup chocolate chips into batter.

3. Spoon batter into prepared muffin cups. Bake 15 to 20 minutes or until toothpicks inserted into centers come out clean. Cool in pans on wire racks 10 minutes. Remove to wire racks; cool completely.

4. Combine frosting and marshmallow creme in medium bowl until well blended. Frost cupcakes.

5. Combine remaining ½ cup chocolate chips and shortening in small microwavable bowl. Microwave at HIGH 30 to 45 seconds, stirring after 30 seconds, or until smooth. Drizzle chocolate mixture over cupcakes. Place one whole cherry on each cupcake.   *Makes 30 cupcakes*

Note: If desired, omit chocolate drizzle and top cupcakes with colored sprinkles.

Chocolate Marbled Blondies

½ cup (1 stick) butter or margarine, softened
½ cup firmly packed light brown sugar
1 large egg
2 teaspoons vanilla extract
1½ cups all-purpose flour
1¼ teaspoons baking soda
1 cup "M&M's"® Chocolate Mini Baking Bits, divided
4 ounces cream cheese, softened
2 tablespoons granulated sugar
1 large egg yolk
¼ cup unsweetened cocoa powder

Preheat oven to 350°F. Lightly grease 9×9×2-inch baking pan; set aside. In large bowl cream butter and brown sugar until light and fluffy; beat in egg and vanilla. In medium bowl combine flour and baking soda; blend into creamed mixture. Stir in ⅔ cup "M&M's"® Chocolate Mini Baking Bits; set aside. Dough will be stiff. In separate bowl beat together cream cheese, granulated sugar and egg yolk until smooth; stir in cocoa powder until well blended. Place chocolate-cheese mixture in six equal portions evenly onto bottom of prepared pan. Place reserved dough around cheese mixture and swirl slightly with tines of fork. Pat down evenly on top. Sprinkle with remaining ⅓ cup "M&M's"® Chocolate Mini Baking Bits. Bake 25 to 30 minutes or until toothpick inserted in center comes out with moist crumbs. Cool completely. Cut into bars. Store in refrigerator in tightly covered container. *Makes 16 bars*

Make It Special

Bring out the creative baker in you with easy-to-make bar cookies. Dazzle cookie monsters with creative cookie treats decorated with brightly colored bits.

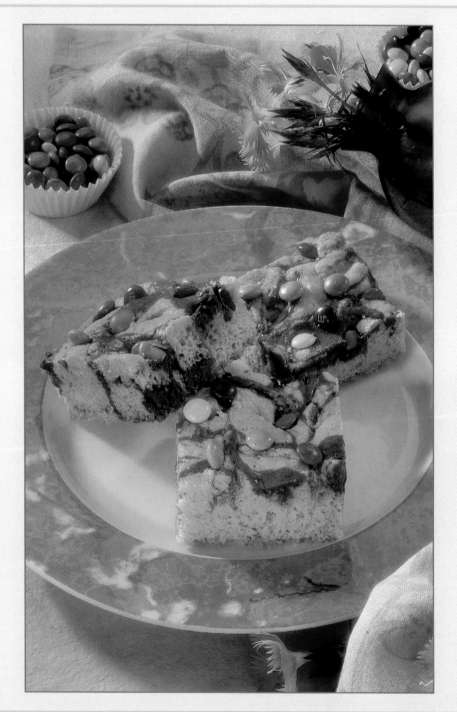

Reese's® Haystacks

1⅔ cups (10-ounce package) REESE'S® Peanut Butter Chips
1 tablespoon shortening (do *not* use butter, margarine, spread or oil)
2½ cups (5-ounce can) chow mein noodles

1. Line tray with wax paper.

2. Place peanut butter chips and shortening in medium microwave-safe bowl. Microwave at HIGH (100%) 1 minute; stir. If necessary, microwave at HIGH an additional 15 seconds at a time, stirring after each heating, just until chips are melted and mixture is smooth when stirred. Immediately add chow mein noodles; stir to coat.

3. Drop mixture by heaping teaspoons onto prepared tray or into paper candy cups. Let stand until firm. If necessary, cover and refrigerate several minutes until firm. Store in tightly covered container. *Makes about 24 treats*

Polar Bear Banana Bites

1 medium banana, cut into 6 equal-size pieces
¼ cup creamy peanut butter*
3 tablespoons fat-free (skim) milk
¼ cup miniature-size marshmallows
2 tablespoons unsalted dry-roasted peanuts, chopped (optional)
1 tablespoon chocolate-flavored decorator sprinkles

Soy butter or almond butter can be used in place of peanut butter.

1. Insert toothpick into each banana piece. Place on tray lined with waxed paper.

2. Whisk together peanut butter and milk. Combine marshmallows, peanuts, if desired, and chocolate sprinkles in shallow dish. Dip each banana piece in peanut butter mixture, draining off excess. Roll in marshmallow mixture. Place on tray; let stand until set.

Makes 6 pieces

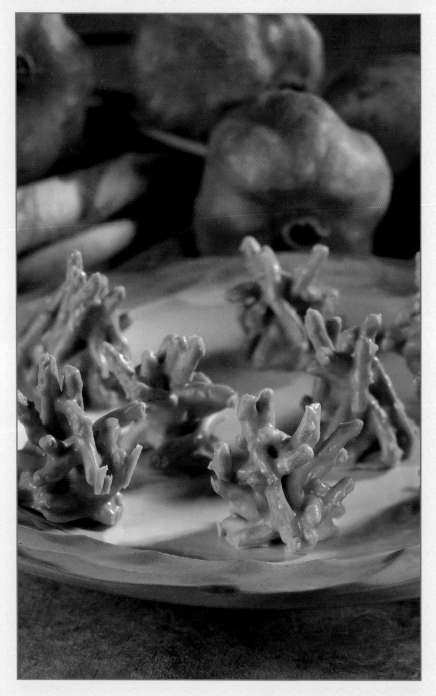

Chocolate Zucchini Snack Cake

1⅔ cups granulated sugar
½ cup (1 stick) butter, softened
½ cup vegetable oil
2 eggs
1½ teaspoons vanilla
2½ cups all-purpose flour
⅓ cup unsweetened cocoa powder
1 teaspoon baking soda
½ teaspoon salt
½ cup buttermilk
2 cups shredded zucchini
¾ cup chopped pecans (optional)
1 cup semisweet chocolate chips

1. Preheat oven to 325°F. Grease and flour 13×9-inch baking pan.

2. Beat sugar, butter and oil in large bowl with electric mixer at medium speed until well blended.

3. Add eggs, one at a time, beating well after each addition. Blend in vanilla.

4. Combine flour, cocoa, baking soda and salt in medium bowl. Add to butter mixture alternately with buttermilk, beating well after each addition. Stir in zucchini.

5. Pour into prepared pan. Sprinkle with pecans, if desired, and chocolate chips.

6. Bake 55 minutes or until toothpick inserted in center comes out clean; cool on wire rack. Cut into squares. *Makes 24 squares*

Chocolate Zucchini Snack Cake ✳ 33

Double Malted Cupcakes

Cupcakes
- 2 cups all-purpose flour
- ¼ cup malted milk powder
- 2 teaspoons baking powder
- ¼ teaspoon salt
- 1¾ cups granulated sugar
- ½ cup (1 stick) butter, softened
- 1 cup reduced-fat (2%) or whole milk
- 1½ teaspoons vanilla
- 3 egg whites

Frosting
- 4 ounces milk chocolate candy bar, broken into chunks
- ¼ cup (½ stick) butter
- ¼ cup whipping cream
- 1 tablespoon malted milk powder
- 1 teaspoon vanilla
- 1¾ cups powdered sugar
- 30 chocolate-covered malt ball candies

1. Preheat oven to 350°F. Line 30 regular-size (2½-inch) muffin cups with paper baking cups.

2. For cupcakes, combine flour, ¼ cup malted milk powder, baking powder and salt; mix well and set aside. Beat sugar and ½ cup butter with electric mixer at medium speed 1 minute. Add milk and 1½ teaspoons vanilla. Beat at low speed 30 seconds. Gradually beat in flour mixture; beat at medium speed 2 minutes. Add egg whites; beat 1 minute.

3. Spoon batter into prepared muffin cups filling ⅔ full. Bake 20 minutes or until golden brown and toothpicks inserted into centers come out clean. Cool in pans on wire racks 10 minutes. (Centers of cupcakes will sink slightly upon cooling.) Remove cupcakes to racks; cool completely. (At this point, cupcakes may be frozen up to 3 months.)

continued on page 36

4. For frosting, melt chocolate and ¼ cup butter in heavy medium saucepan over low heat, stirring frequently. Stir in cream, 1 tablespoon malted milk powder and 1 teaspoon vanilla; mix well. Gradually stir in powdered sugar. Cook 4 to 5 minutes, stirring constantly, until small lumps disappear. Remove from heat. Refrigerate 20 minutes, beating every 5 minutes or until frosting is spreadable.

5. Spread cooled cupcakes with frosting; decorate with chocolate-covered malt ball candies. Store at room temperature up to 24 hours or cover and refrigerate for up to 3 days before serving.

Makes 30 cupcakes

Monkey Bars

    3 cups miniature marshmallows
    ½ cup honey
    ⅓ cup butter
    ¼ cup peanut butter
    2 teaspoons vanilla
    ¼ teaspoon salt
    4 cups crispy rice cereal
    2 cups rolled oats, uncooked
    ½ cup flaked coconut
    ¼ cup peanuts

Combine marshmallows, honey, butter, peanut butter, vanilla and salt in medium saucepan. Melt marshmallow mixture over low heat, stirring constantly. Combine rice cereal, oats, coconut and peanuts in 13×9×2-inch baking pan. Pour marshmallow mixture over dry ingredients. Mix until thoroughly coated. Press mixture firmly into pan. Cool completely before cutting. *Makes 24 bars*

Microwave Directions: Microwave marshmallows, honey, butter, peanut butter, vanilla and salt in 2-quart microwave-safe bowl on HIGH 2½ to 3 minutes. Continue as above.

Favorite recipe from **National Honey Board**

Mini Turtle Cupcakes

  1 **package (21.5 ounces) brownie mix plus ingredients
     to prepare mix**
  ½ **cup chopped pecans (optional)**
  1 **cup prepared or homemade dark chocolate frosting**
  ½ **cup coarsely chopped pecans, toasted (optional)**
 12 **caramels**
  1 **to 2 tablespoons whipping cream**

1. Heat oven to 350°F. Line 54 mini (1½-inch) muffin cups with paper baking cups.

2. Prepare brownie batter as directed on package. Stir in chopped pecans, if desired.

3. Spoon batter into prepared muffin cups filling ⅔ full. Bake 18 minutes or until toothpicks inserted into centers come out clean. Cool in pans on wire racks 5 minutes. Remove cupcakes to racks; cool completely. (At this point, cupcakes may be frozen up to 3 months. Thaw at room temperature before frosting.)

4. Spread frosting over cooled cupcakes; top with toasted pecans, if desired.

5. Combine caramels and 1 tablespoon cream in small saucepan. Cook and stir over low heat until caramels are melted and mixture is smooth. Add additional 1 tablespoon cream if needed. Spoon caramel decoratively over cupcakes. Store at room temperature up to 24 hours or cover and refrigerate for up to 3 days before serving.

Makes 54 mini cupcakes

Mini Pizza Cookies

1 20-ounce tube refrigerated sugar cookie dough
2 cups (16 ounces) prepared pink frosting
  "M&M's"® Chocolate Mini Baking Bits
  Variety of additional toppings such as shredded coconut,
    granola, raisins, nuts, small pretzels, snack mixes, sunflower
    seeds, popped corn and mini marshmallows

Preheat oven to 350°F. Lightly grease cookie sheets; set aside. Divide dough into 8 equal portions. On lightly floured surface, roll each portion of dough into ¼-inch-thick circle; place circles about 2 inches apart onto prepared cookie sheets. Bake 10 to 13 minutes or until golden brown on edges. Cool completely on wire racks. Spread top of each pizza with frosting; sprinkle with "M&M's"® Chocolate Mini Baking Bits and 2 or 3 suggested toppings.   *Makes 8 large cookies*

Summer Fruits with Peanut Butter-Honey Dip

⅓ cup smooth or chunky peanut butter
2 tablespoons milk
2 tablespoons honey
1 tablespoon apple juice or water
⅛ teaspoon ground cinnamon
2 cups melon balls, including cantaloupe and honeydew
1 peach or nectarine, pitted and cut into 8 wedges
1 banana, peeled and thickly sliced

1. Place peanut butter in small bowl; gradually stir in milk and honey until blended. Stir in apple juice and cinnamon until mixture is smooth.

2. Serve dip along with prepared fruits.
                    Makes 4 servings (about ½ cup dip)

Prep Time: 20 minutes

Ultimate Rocky Road Cups

¾ **cup (1½ sticks) butter or margarine**
4 **squares (1 ounce each) unsweetened baking chocolate**
1½ **cups granulated sugar**
3 **large eggs**
1 **cup all-purpose flour**
1¾ **cups "M&M's"® Chocolate Mini Baking Bits**
¾ **cup coarsely chopped peanuts (optional)**
1 **cup mini marshmallows**

Preheat oven to 350°F. Generously grease 24 (2½-inch) muffin cups or line with foil liners. Place butter and chocolate in large microwave-safe bowl. Microwave on HIGH 1 minute; stir. Microwave on HIGH an additional 30 seconds; stir until chocolate is completely melted. Add sugar and eggs, one at a time, beating well after each addition; blend in flour. In separate bowl combine "M&M's"® Chocolate Mini Baking Bits and nuts, if desired; stir 1 cup baking bits mixture into brownie batter. Divide batter evenly among prepared muffin cups. Bake 20 minutes. Combine remaining baking bits mixture with marshmallows; divide evenly among muffin cups, topping hot brownies. Return to oven; bake 5 minutes longer. Cool completely before removing from muffin cups. Store in tightly covered container. *Makes 24 cups*

Mini Ultimate Rocky Road Cups: Prepare recipe as directed, dividing batter among 60 generously greased 2-inch mini muffin cups. Bake 15 minutes. Sprinkle with topping mixture; bake 5 minutes longer. Cool completely before removing from cups. Store in tightly covered container. Makes about 60 mini cups.

Ultimate Rocky Road Squares: Prepare recipe as directed, spreading batter into generously greased 13×9×2-inch baking pan. Bake 30 minutes. Sprinkle with topping mixture; bake 5 minutes longer. Cool completely. Cut into squares. Store in tightly covered container. Makes 24 squares.

Red's Rockin' Rainbow Cupcakes

2¼ cups all-purpose flour
1 tablespoon baking powder
½ teaspoon salt
1⅔ cups granulated sugar
½ cup (1 stick) butter, softened
1 cup milk
2 teaspoons vanilla extract
3 large egg whites
  Blue and assorted food colorings
1 container (16 ounces) white frosting
1½ cups "M&M's"® Chocolate Mini Baking Bits, divided

Preheat oven to 350°F. Lightly grease 24 (2¾-inch) muffin cups or line with paper or foil liners; set aside. In large bowl combine flour, baking powder and salt. Blend in sugar, butter, milk and vanilla; beat about 2 minutes. Add egg whites; beat 2 minutes. Divide batter evenly among prepared muffin cups. Place 2 drops desired food coloring into each muffin cup. Swirl gently with knife. Sprinkle evenly with ¾ cup "M&M's"® Chocolate Mini Baking Bits. Bake 20 to 25 minutes or until toothpick inserted in centers comes out clean. Cool completely on wire racks. Combine frosting and blue food coloring. Spread frosting over cupcakes; decorate with remaining ¾ cup "M&M's"® Chocolate Mini Baking Bits to make rainbows. Store in tightly covered container.

Makes 24 cupcakes

Tasty Teaching Tip

Make learning fun by letting kids decorate a cupcake or cookie with tubes of frosting, colorful candies or any edible decoration. Decorating activities can be fantastic opportunities for learning colors and numbers.

Inside-Out Peanut Butter Cookie Sandwiches

1¼ cups all-purpose flour
½ teaspoon baking soda
½ teaspoon salt
¾ cup (1½ sticks) butter, softened
⅔ cup creamy or chunky peanut butter
½ cup granulated sugar
½ cup packed brown sugar
1 large egg
1¾ cups (10-ounce package) NESTLÉ® TOLL HOUSE® Holiday
    Shapes & Morsels, *divided*
    Peanut Butter Frosting and Filling (recipe follows)

PREHEAT oven to 350°F.

COMBINE flour, baking soda and salt in small bowl. Beat butter, peanut butter, granulated sugar, brown sugar and vanilla extract in large mixer bowl until creamy. Beat in egg. Gradually beat in flour mixture. *Stir in 1 cup Shapes & Morsels (set aside remaining Shapes & Morsels).* Drop dough by rounded tablespoon onto ungreased baking sheets. Press down slightly.

BAKE for 10 to 13 minutes or until golden brown. Cool on baking sheets on wire racks for 2 minutes; remove to wire racks to cool completely.

SPREAD Peanut Butter Frosting and Filling on bottom side of one cookie. Place bottom side of a second cookie over frosting creating a cookie sandwich; press down slightly. Frost top of cookie sandwich and *sprinkle with remaining Shapes & Morsels.* Repeat with *remaining* cookies.   *Makes about 20 cookie sandwiches*

Peanut Butter Frosting and Filling: Stir together 1¼ cups prepared vanilla frosting and ¼ cup creamy or chunky peanut butter.

Peanut Butter Chips and Jelly Bars

1½ **cups all-purpose flour**
½ **cup sugar**
¾ **teaspoon baking powder**
½ **cup (1 stick) cold butter or margarine**
1 **egg, beaten**
¾ **cup grape jelly**
1⅔ **cups (10-ounce package) REESE'S® Peanut Butter Chips, divided**

1. Heat oven to 375°F. Grease 9-inch square baking pan.

2. Stir together flour, sugar and baking powder in large bowl. With pastry blender or two knives, cut in butter until mixture resembles coarse crumbs. Add egg; blend well. Reserve 1 cup mixture; press remaining mixture onto bottom of prepared pan. Stir jelly to soften; spread evenly over crust. Sprinkle 1 cup peanut butter chips over jelly. Stir together reserved crumb mixture with remaining ⅔ cup chips; sprinkle over top.

3. Bake 25 to 30 minutes or until lightly browned. Cool completely in pan on wire rack. Cut into bars. *Makes about 16 bars*

Make It Special

Serve the best-shaped cookies in town. Use cookie cutters to cut out shapes from these and other bars cookies for a whimsical twist. Make shapes like stars, circles, letters or the school mascot to suit your party theme.

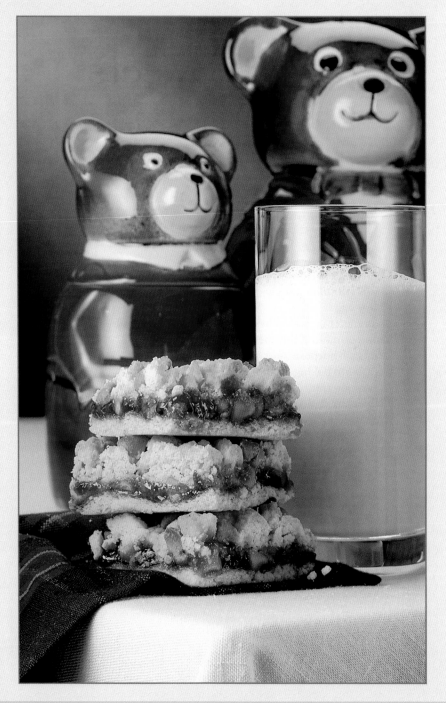

Novelty Sweets

Journey to the land of make-believe where simple cakes and cookies are transformed into stunning creations. Kids' eyes will light up with excitement when they discover these special-shaped, colorfully decorated treats.

Dino-Mite Dinosaurs

    1 cup (2 sticks) butter, softened
1¼ cups granulated sugar
    1 large egg
    2 squares (1 ounce each) semi-sweet chocolate, melted
    ½ teaspoon vanilla extract
2⅓ cups all-purpose flour
    1 teaspoon baking powder
    ¼ teaspoon salt
    1 cup white frosting
       Assorted food colorings
    1 cup "M&M's"® Chocolate Mini Baking Bits

In large bowl cream butter and sugar until light and fluffy; beat in egg, chocolate and vanilla. In medium bowl combine flour, baking powder and salt; add to creamed mixture. Wrap and refrigerate dough 2 to 3 hours. Preheat oven to 350°F. Working with half the dough at a time on lightly floured surface, roll to ¼-inch thickness. Cut into dinosaur shapes using 4-inch cookie cutters. Place about 2 inches apart on ungreased cookie sheets. Bake 10 to 12 minutes. Cool 2 minutes on cookie sheets; cool completely on wire racks. Tint frosting to desired colors. Frost cookies and decorate with "M&M's"® Chocolate Mini Baking Bits. Store in tightly covered container.   *Makes 24 cookies*

Juke Box Cake

1 package (about 18 ounces) chocolate fudge cake mix, plus ingredients to prepare mix
1 container (16 ounces) buttercream frosting, divided
Red and yellow food coloring
1 container (12 ounces) whipped milk chocolate frosting
1 tube (4¼ ounces) black decorating icing plus plain decorating tip

1. Preheat oven to 350°F. Grease and flour 13×9-inch cake pan; set aside.

2. Prepare cake mix according to package directions. Pour batter evenly into prepared pan. Bake 35 minutes or until wooden pick inserted into center comes out clean.

3. Cool cake in pan on wire rack 10 minutes. Remove cake to wire rack; cool completely.

4. Meanwhile, color frostings. Place ¼ cup buttercream frosting in small bowl; tint red with red food coloring (about 20 drops). In another small bowl, add ¼ cup buttercream frosting; tint orange using 6 drops red and 8 drops yellow food coloring. Place each in pastry bags fitted with plain tips (#5 or 6) or resealable plastic food storage bags with 1 corner cut off.

5. Using paper plate as a guide, cut top of juke box into rounded shape. (Refer to diagram.)

6. Frost entire cake with chocolate frosting. Use some of remaining buttercream frosting to create semicircular background for records and wedge-shaped background for speakers. Using orange frosting, pipe small section above semicircle and grate on speaker section.

7. Place remaining buttercream frosting into pastry bag fitted with basket weave tip (#48); pipe 2 panels between record area and speaker section.

8. Use black decorating icing fitted with plain decorating tip to add additional details.

9. Pipe red and orange stripes around edges of juke box. *Makes 20 servings*

Mice Creams

1 pint vanilla ice cream
1 (4-ounce) package READY CRUST® Mini-Graham Cracker
    Pie Crusts
    Ears—12 KEEBLER® Grasshopper® cookies
    Tails—3 chocolate twigs, broken in half *or* 6 (3-inch) pieces
    black shoestring licorice
    Eyes and noses—18 brown candy-coated chocolate candies
    Whiskers—2 teaspoons chocolate sprinkles

Place 1 scoop vanilla ice cream into each crust. Press cookie ears and tails into ice cream. Press eyes, noses, and whiskers in place. Serve immediately. Do not refreeze. *Makes 6 servings*

Prep Time: 15 minutes

Leapin' Lizards!

1 cup butterscotch-flavor chips
½ cup corn syrup
3 tablespoons butter
1 cup white chocolate chips
    Green food coloring
7 cups crisp rice cereal
    Candy corn, green jelly beans, red miniature jaw breakers
    and chocolate chips

1. Line baking sheet with waxed paper.

2. Combine butterscotch chips, corn syrup and butter in large saucepan. Stir over medium heat until chips are melted. Add white chocolate chips and green food coloring; stir well. Remove from heat. Add cereal; stir to coat evenly.

3. Lightly butter hands and shape about 1½ cups cereal mixture into lizard (about 6 inches long). Place on prepared baking sheet. Decorate with candies. Repeat with remaining mixture. *Makes 4 lizards*

Sunshine Butter Cookies

¾ cup (1½ sticks) butter, softened
¾ cup sugar
1 egg
2¼ cups all-purpose flour
¼ teaspoon salt
Grated peel of ½ lemon
1 teaspoon frozen lemonade concentrate, thawed
Lemonade Royal Icing (recipe page 56)
Thin pretzel sticks
Yellow paste food coloring
Gummy fruit and black licorice strings

1. Beat butter and sugar in large bowl at high speed of electric mixer until fluffy. Add egg; beat well.

2. Combine flour, salt and lemon peel in medium bowl. Add to butter mixture. Stir in lemonade concentrate. Refrigerate 2 hours.

3. Prepare Lemonade Royal Icing. Cover; let stand at room temperature. Preheat oven to 350°F. Grease cookie sheets.

4. Roll dough on floured surface to ⅛-inch thickness. Cut out cookies using 3-inch round cookie cutter. Place cookies on prepared cookie sheets. Press pretzel sticks into edges of cookies to resemble sunshine rays; press gently. Bake 10 minutes or until lightly browned. Remove to wire racks; cool completely.

5. Add food coloring to Lemonade Royal Icing. Spoon about ½ cup icing into resealable plastic food storage bag; seal. Cut tiny tip from corner of bag. Pipe thin circle around flat side of each cookie to create outline.

6. Add water, 1 tablespoon at a time, to remaining icing in bowl until thick but pourable consistency. Spoon icing in cookie centers staying within outline.

7. Decorate cookies with gummy fruit and licorice to make "sunny" faces. Let stand 1 hour or until dry.   *Makes about 36 cookies*

continued on page 56

Lemonade Royal Icing

3¾ **cups sifted powdered sugar**
  3 **tablespoons meringue powder**
  6 **tablespoons frozen lemonade concentrate, thawed**

Beat all ingredients in large bowl at high speed of electric mixer until smooth.

Ghosts on a Stick

4 **wooden craft sticks**
4 **medium pears, stems removed**
9 **squares (2 ounces each) almond bark**
  Mini chocolate chips

● Line baking sheet with waxed paper and 4 paper baking cups. Insert wooden sticks into stem ends of pears.

● Melt almond bark according to package directions.

● Dip one pear into melted almond bark, spooning bark over top to coat evenly. Remove excess by scraping pear bottom across rim of measuring cup. Place on paper baking cup; let set 1 minute.

● Decorate with mini chocolate chips to make ghost face. Repeat with remaining pears. Place spoonful of extra almond bark at bottom of pears for ghost tails. Refrigerate until firm. *Makes 4 servings*

ABC Cookies

½ cup (1 stick) butter, softened
½ cup granulated sugar
1 large egg
2 tablespoons orange juice
1½ cups all-purpose flour
1 teaspoon grated orange peel
½ teaspoon baking powder
⅛ teaspoon salt
Orange Icing (recipe follows)
1 cup "M&M's"® Chocolate Mini Baking Bits

In large bowl cream butter and sugar until light and fluffy; beat in egg and orange juice. In medium bowl combine flour, orange peel, baking powder and salt; add to creamed mixture. Wrap and refrigerate dough 2 to 3 hours. Preheat oven to 350°F. Working with half the dough at a time on well-floured surface, roll to ¼-inch thickness. Cut into letter shapes using 1½-inch cookie cutters. Place about 2 inches apart on ungreased cookie sheets. Bake 8 to 10 minutes. Cool 1 minute on cookie sheets; cool completely on wire racks. Prepare Orange Icing; spread over cookies. Decorate with "M&M's"® Chocolate Mini Baking Bits. Store in tightly covered container.   *Makes about 84 cookies*

Orange Icing: In medium bowl combine 1 cup powdered sugar, 1 tablespoon water and 1 tablespoon pulp-free orange juice. Add additional water, 1 teaspoon at a time, if necessary to make icing spreadable.

Save Time

You can find specialty cookie cutters in the cake decorating section of craft stores. If you are in a hurry, cut the dough into circles or squares. Bake and frost as above. Then use tubes of colorful frosting to print names, letters or numbers on the top.

Ice Cream Cone Cakes

1 package DUNCAN HINES® Moist Deluxe® Cake Mix (any flavor)
1 container DUNCAN HINES® Creamy Home-Style Chocolate Frosting
1 container DUNCAN HINES® Creamy Home-Style Vanilla Frosting
Chocolate sprinkles
Assorted decors
Jelly beans
2 maraschino cherries, for garnish

1. Preheat oven to 350°F. Grease and flour one 8-inch round cake pan and one 8-inch square pan.

2. Prepare cake following package directions for basic recipe. Pour about 2 cups batter into round pan. Pour about 3 cups batter into square pan. Bake at 350°F for 30 to 35 minutes or until toothpick inserted in center comes out clean. Cool following package directions.

3. To assemble, cut cooled cake and arrange as shown. Frost "cone" with Chocolate frosting, reserving ½ cup. Place writing tip in pastry bag. Fill with remaining ½ cup Chocolate frosting. Pipe waffle pattern onto "cones." Decorate with chocolate sprinkles. Spread Vanilla frosting on "ice cream." Decorate with assorted decors and jelly beans. Top each with maraschino cherry.   *Makes 12 to 16 servings*

Tip: Use tip of knife to draw lines in frosting for waffle pattern as guide for piping chocolate frosting.

Igloo Cake

1 package (about 18 ounces) white cake mix plus
   ingredients to prepare mix
1 cup marshmallow creme
1 container (16 ounces) white frosting, divided
1 snack-size plain cake donut
  Blue food coloring
  White cake glitter
  Rock candy
  Plastic polar bear and penguin figurines (optional)

1. Preheat oven to 350°F. Grease and lightly flour 8-inch heatproof ceramic or metal mixing bowl.

2. Prepare cake mix according to package directions. Pour batter evenly into bowl. Bake 50 to 55 minutes or until cake tester or bamboo skewer inserted into center of cake comes out clean.

3. Cool in pan on wire rack 10 minutes. Remove cake to wire rack; cool completely.

4. Using serrated knife, divide cake horizontally into 2 layers. Place bottom layer on serving plate.

5. Using long spatula lightly sprayed with cooking spray, spread marshmallow creme on bottom cake layer to within ½ inch of edge. Stack top cake layer on top.

6. Remove ¼ cup frosting from container; set aside. Use most of remaining frosting to frost cake. Attach donut to base of cake to form entrance to igloo; frost completely.

7. Color reserved frosting with blue food coloring and place in a pastry bag fitted with #7 plain tip. Pipe frosting in circular strips around cake, 2 inches apart. Pipe short, vertical strips between horizontal strips to give illusion of blocks of ice. Pipe doorway onto frosted donut.

8. Dust cake with cake glitter to resemble snow. Break chunks of rock candy and scatter around outside of cake. Decorate with plastic polar bear and penguin figurines, if desired. *Makes 16 to 20 servings*

Purse Cake

1 package (about 18 ounces) yellow cake mix, plus ingredients
   to prepare mix
½ cup seedless raspberry preserves
1 container (16 ounces) white frosting
   Red food coloring
   Assorted candies: black string licorice, soft licorice pieces, black
      jelly beans, pastel egg sprinkles, candy bracelet, candy crayons

1. Preheat oven to 350°F. Grease and flour 13×9-inch cake pan; set aside.

2. Prepare cake mix according to package directions. Pour batter
evenly into prepared pan. Bake 35 minutes or until wooden pick
inserted into center of cake comes out clean.

3. Cool in pan on wire rack 10 minutes. Remove cake from pan to wire
rack; cool completely.

4. Use wooden picks to mark sections to be cut (Diagram A). Use
serrated knife to cut cake into 4 sections. Discard ½-inch strip of excess
cake.

continued on page 64

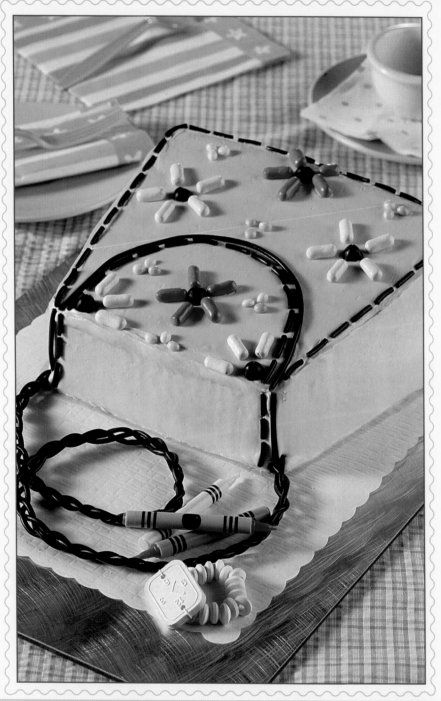

Purse Cake, continued

5. Place widest section (Piece 1), cut side down, on cake board or serving platter. Spread left side of Piece 1 with preserves; attach next-widest section (Piece 2), cut side down, to the left of Piece 1 so layers are stacked sideways. Repeat process for remaining 2 sections. Final cake should gradually slope downward from right to left (Diagram B).

6. Measure 1 inch from side of shortest cake section. Using serrated knife, cut back to corner of tallest section. Repeat on other side of cake. Discard scraps (Diagram C). Cover cake with foil or plastic wrap and freeze several hours before frosting.

7. Tint frosting pink using red food coloring. Remove cake from freezer; frost cake on all sides, filling in graduated slope with frosting.

8. To decorate cake, cut 18-inch piece black string licorice; gently press into frosting to outline purse flap. Cut ½-inch pieces to resemble stitching. Use 5 pink or white licorice candies to create flower petals. Place halved black jelly bean in center of each flower. Place pastel egg sprinkles in groups of 3 to add more texture. To make purse strap, knot 3 long pieces string licorice together. Braid licorice; knot other end. Push knots into frosting on sides of purse. Place candy crayons and bracelets around purse.   *Makes 16 to 20 servings*

Make It Special

In addition to traditional birthday candles, decorate cakes with a variety of candies and chocolates such as licorice whips, milk chocolate buttons, rainbow sprinkles, candy-covered chocolates, white chocolate chips, chocolate numbers, glacé cherries and other assorted candies or nonpareils. Use candies to transform plain cakes into realistic pictures.

Shapers

2 packages (20 ounces each) refrigerated sugar cookie dough
Red, yellow, green and blue paste food colorings
1 container (16 ounces) vanilla frosting

1. Remove dough from wrapper according to package directions. Cut each roll of dough in half.

2. Beat ¼ of dough and red food coloring in medium bowl until well blended. Shape red dough into 5-inch log on sheet of waxed paper; set aside.

3. Repeat with remaining dough and food colorings. Cover; refrigerate tinted logs 1 hour or until firm.

4. Roll or shape each log on smooth surface to create circular, triangular, square and oval-shaped logs. Use ruler to keep triangle and square sides flat. Cover; refrigerate dough 1 hour or until firm.

5. Preheat oven to 350°F. Cut shaped dough into ¼-inch slices. Place 2 inches apart on ungreased baking sheets. Bake 9 to 12 minutes. Remove to wire racks; cool completely.

6. Spoon frosting into resealable plastic food storage bag; seal. Cut tiny tip from corner of bag. Pipe frosting around each cookie to define shape.

Makes about 80 cookies

Make It Special

If you have extra liquid food colorings at home, tint the vanilla frosting different colors. Frost cookies using contrasting colored frosting, for example green frosting on a red cookie.

Chocolate X and O Cookies

⅔ cup butter or margarine, softened
1 cup sugar
2 teaspoons vanilla extract
2 eggs
2 tablespoons light corn syrup
2½ cups all-purpose flour
½ cup HERSHEY'S Cocoa
½ teaspoon baking soda
¼ teaspoon salt
Decorating icing

1. Beat butter, sugar and vanilla in large bowl on medium speed of electric mixer until fluffy. Add eggs; beat well. Beat in corn syrup.

2. Combine flour, cocoa, baking soda and salt; gradually add to butter mixture, beating until well blended. Cover; refrigerate until dough is firm enough to handle.

3. Heat oven to 350°F. Shape dough into X and O shapes. Place on ungreased cookie sheet.

4. Bake 5 minutes or until set. Remove from cookie sheet to wire rack. Cool completely. Decorate as desired with icing.

Makes about 60 cookies

Preparation Hint

To shape X's: Shape rounded teaspoons of dough into 3-inch logs. Place 1 log on cookie sheet; press lightly in center. Place another 3-inch log on top of first one, forming X shape. To shape O's: Shape rounded teaspoon dough into 5-inch logs. Connect ends, pressing lightly, forming O shape.

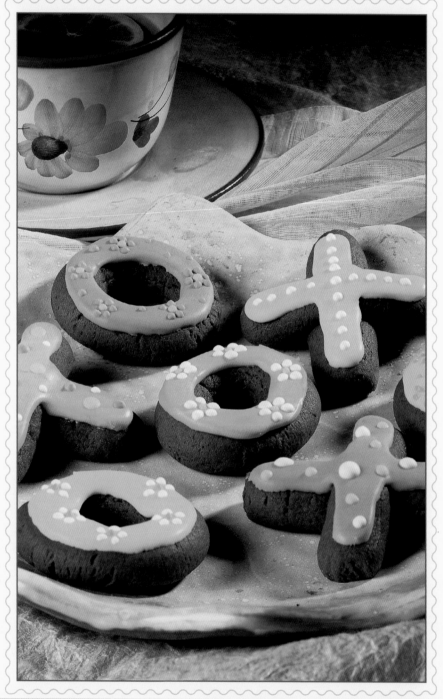

Drum Layer Cake

1 package DUNCAN HINES® Moist Deluxe® Cake Mix (any flavor)
1 container DUNCAN HINES® Creamy Home-Style Classic Vanilla
   Frosting, divided
Green food coloring
Thin pretzel sticks
Candy-coated chocolate pieces
Lollipops

1. Preheat oven to 350°F. Grease and flour two 8-inch round cake pans.

2. Prepare, bake and cool cake following package directions for basic recipe.

3. To assemble, place half the Vanilla frosting in small bowl. Tint with green food coloring; set aside. Place one cake layer on serving plate. Spread with half of untinted vanilla frosting. Top with second cake layer. Spread green frosting on sides of cake. Spread remaining Vanilla frosting on top of cake. Arrange pretzel sticks and candy-coated chocolates on sides of cake as shown in photograph. Place lollipops on top of cake for "drumsticks."   *Makes 12 to 16 servings*

Preparation Hint

For a brighter green frosting, as shown in the photograph, use paste food colors available from cake decorating and specialty shops.

Stripes

5½ cups cake batter, divided
1 (10-inch) round cake board, covered, or large platter
1 container (16 ounces) white frosting
3 chocolate sandwich cookies
1 individual chocolate-covered cake roll
   Pretzel sticks
   Chocolate sprinkles
   Assorted candies and red licorice whip

1. Preheat oven to 350°F. Grease and flour 9-inch round cake pan and medium muffin pan.

2. Pour 3½ cups cake batter into cake pan; pour remaining cake batter into muffin pan (¼ cup batter per muffin cup). Bake cake in pan 35 to 45 minutes and cupcakes about 20 minutes or until toothpick inserted into centers comes out clean. Cool 15 minutes in pans. Loosen edges; invert onto wire racks and cool completely.

3. Trim tops and sides of round cake and two cupcakes. (Reserve remaining cupcakes for another use.) Place cake on prepared cake board. Position two cupcakes next to cake to form ears.

4. Tint frosting orange. Frost entire cake and cupcakes with orange frosting.

5. Carefully open two sandwich cookies to expose white filling. Place opened cookies on tiger's ears. Cut two thin slices from cake roll; place on tiger's face for eyes.

6. Add pretzel whiskers, cookie nose, candy mouth and chocolate sprinkle stripes as shown in photo.   *Makes 12 to 14 servings*

Holiday Celebrations

Celebrate holidays throughout the year with whimsical, festive treats that fascinate and delight. Draw rave reviews with these fabulous ideas—perfect for any school holiday party.

Cookie Decorating Party

1 container (16 ounces) strawberry frosting, at room temperature
48 vanilla wafers or sugar cookies
¼ to ½ pound assorted Valentine candies, such as cinnamon hearts, conversation hearts, chocolate candies, red hots and heart-shaped sprinkles

Stir frosting in can until soft and creamy. Divide frosting evenly among small paper cups to equal one paper cup per child. Give each child an equal number of cookies, one paper cup of frosting and assortment of candies. Have children dip cookies into frosting or spread frosting with backs of spoons. Decorate with candies or sprinkles as desired.

Makes 48 cookies

Make It Special

Create your own decorating party for any holiday or birthday. Use different colored frostings, holiday candies and fun sprinkles to create themed cookies for every occasion.

Valentine Stained Glass Hearts

½ **cup (1 stick) butter or margarine, softened**
¾ **cup granulated sugar**
2 **eggs**
1 **teaspoon vanilla extract**
2⅓ **cups all-purpose flour**
1 **teaspoon baking powder**
   Red hard candies, crushed (about ⅓ cup)
   Frosting (optional)

Cream butter and sugar in mixing bowl. Beat in eggs and vanilla. Sift flour and baking powder together. Gradually stir in flour mixture until dough is very stiff. Cover and chill. Dough needs to chill 3 hours to overnight.

Preheat oven to 375°F. Roll out dough to ⅛-inch thickness on lightly floured surface. To prevent cookies from becoming tough and brittle, do not incorporate too much flour. Cut out cookies using large heart-shaped cookie cutter or use sharp knife and cut heart design. Transfer cookies to foil-lined baking sheet. Using small heart-shaped cookie cutter, cut out and remove heart design from center of each cookie. Fill cutout sections with crushed candy. Bake 7 to 9 minutes or until cookies are lightly browned and candy has melted. Do not overcook.

Remove from oven; immediately slide foil off baking sheet. Cool completely; carefully loosen cookies from foil. If desired, pipe decorative borders with frosting around edges.

Makes about 30 cookies

Favorite recipe from **The Sugar Association, Inc.**

Irish Flag Cookies

1½ **cups all-purpose flour**
1 **teaspoon baking powder**
½ **teaspoon salt**
¾ **cup granulated sugar**
¾ **cup light brown sugar**
½ **cup (1 stick) butter, softened**
2 **eggs**
2 **teaspoons vanilla**
1 **package (12 ounces) semisweet chocolate chips**
Prepared white frosting
Green and orange food coloring

1. Preheat oven to 350°F. Grease 13×9-inch baking pan. Combine flour, baking powder and salt in small bowl; set aside.

2. Beat granulated sugar, brown sugar and butter in large bowl with electric mixer at medium speed until light and fluffy. Beat in eggs and vanilla. Add flour mixture. Beat at low speed until well blended. Stir in chocolate chips. Spread batter evenly into prepared pan. Bake 25 to 30 minutes or until golden brown. Remove pan to wire rack; cool completely. Cut into 3¼×1½-inch bars.

3. Divide frosting among 3 small bowls. Tint 1 with green food coloring and 1 with orange. Leave remaining frosting white. Frost individual cookies to resemble the Irish flag as shown in diagram.

Makes 24 cookies

St. Pat's Pudding Pies

1 package (4-serving size) pistachio pudding and pie filling
    mix plus ingredients to prepare mix
1 package mini graham cracker pie crusts (6 crusts)
    Assorted candies, colored sprinkles and gumdrops

Prepare pudding according to package directions; divide evenly among crusts. Decorate with candies and sprinkles as desired. Roll gumdrops on heavily sugared surface until fairly flat; cut into shamrock shapes. Place in centers of pies. Refrigerate leftovers. *Makes 6 pies*

Chocolate Bunny Cookies

1 (21-ounce) package DUNCAN HINES® Family-Style
    Chewy Fudge Brownie Mix
1 egg
¼ cup water
¼ cup vegetable oil
1⅓ cups pecan halves (96)
1 container DUNCAN HINES® Creamy Home-Style
    Dark Chocolate Fudge Frosting
    White chocolate chips

1. Preheat oven to 350°F. Grease baking sheets.

2. Combine brownie mix, egg, water and oil in large bowl. Stir with spoon until well blended, about 50 strokes. Drop by level tablespoonfuls 2 inches apart on greased baking sheets. Place two pecan halves, flat-side up, on each cookie for ears. Bake at 350°F for 10 to 12 minutes or until set. Cool 2 minutes on baking sheets. Remove to cooling racks. Cool completely.

3. Spread Dark Chocolate Fudge frosting on one cookie. Place white chocolate chips, upside down, on frosting for eyes and nose. Dot each eye with frosting using toothpick. Repeat for remaining cookies. Allow frosting to set before storing cookies between layers of waxed paper in airtight container. *Makes 48 cookies*

Tip: For variety, frost cookies with Duncan Hines® Vanilla Frosting and use semisweet chocolate chips for the eyes and noses.

Eggs-Cellent Easter Cookies

1 package (18 ounces) refrigerated sugar cookie dough
1 cup plus 1 tablespoon powdered sugar, divided
¼ cup all-purpose flour
1 teaspoon almond extract
   Blue food coloring
   Blue sugar (optional)
1 package (3 ounces) cream cheese, softened
1 tablespoon unsalted butter, softened
   Red food coloring
½ cup shredded sweetened coconut (optional)
   Prepared colored decorating icings and decorating gels
      (optional)

1. Preheat oven to 350°F. Grease cookie sheets. Remove dough from wrapper; place in large bowl. Let dough stand at room temperature about 15 minutes.

2. Add 1 tablespoon powdered sugar, flour, almond extract and blue food coloring to dough in bowl; beat at medium speed of electric mixer until well blended and evenly colored.

3. Shape dough into 40 (2½-inch-long) egg shapes; roll in blue sugar, if desired. Place 2 inches apart on prepared cookie sheets.

4. Bake 8 to 10 minutes or until set and edges are lightly browned. Cool on cookie sheets 2 minutes. Remove to wire racks; cool completely.

5. Combine cream cheese, butter, remaining 1 cup powdered sugar and red food coloring (tint pink) in medium bowl; beat at medium speed of electric mixer until smooth. Stir in coconut, if desired.

6. Spread pink filling on 20 cookies. Top with remaining 20 cookies to make sandwiches. Decorate tops of sandwiches as desired with colored icings and gels. Let stand until set. Store in refrigerator.

Makes 20 sandwich cookies

Easter Baskets and Bunnies Cupcakes

　　2 cups sugar
1¾ cups all-purpose flour
　¾ cup HERSHEY'S Cocoa or HERSHEY'S Dutch Processed Cocoa
1½ teaspoons baking powder
1½ teaspoons baking soda
　1 teaspoon salt
　2 eggs
　1 cup milk
　½ cup vegetable oil
　2 teaspoons vanilla extract
　1 cup boiling water
　　Creamy Vanilla Frosting (recipe follows)
　　Green, red and yellow food color
3¾ cups MOUNDS® Sweetened Coconut Flakes, divided and tinted*
　　Suggested garnishes (marshmallows, HERSHEY'S MINI KISSES™
　　　Milk Chocolates, licorice, jelly beans)

To tint coconut, combine ¾ teaspoon water with several drops green food color in small bowl. Stir in 1¼ cups coconut. Toss with fork until evenly tinted. Repeat with red and yellow food color and remaining coconut.

1. Heat oven to 350°F. Line muffin cups (2½ inches in diameter) with paper bake cups.

2. Stir together sugar, flour, cocoa, baking powder, baking soda and salt in large bowl. Add eggs, milk, oil and vanilla; beat on medium speed of mixer 2 minutes. Stir in boiling water (batter will be thin). Fill muffin cups ⅔ full with batter.

3. Bake 22 to 25 minutes or until wooden pick inserted in centers comes out clean. Cool completely. Prepare Creamy Vanilla Frosting; frost cupcakes. Immediately press desired color tinted coconut onto each cupcake. Garnish as desired to resemble Easter basket or bunny.

Makes about 33 cupcakes

Creamy Vanilla Frosting: Beat ⅓ cup softened butter or margarine in medium bowl. Add 1 cup powdered sugar and 1½ teaspoons vanilla extract; beat well. Add 2½ cups powdered sugar alternately with ¼ cup milk, beating to spreading consistency. Makes about 2 cups frosting.

Patriotic Cocoa Cupcakes

　　2 cups sugar
　1¾ cups all-purpose flour
　　¾ cup HERSHEY'S Cocoa
　　2 teaspoons baking soda
　　1 teaspoon baking powder
　　1 teaspoon salt
　　2 eggs
　　1 cup buttermilk or sour milk*
　　1 cup boiling water
　　½ cup vegetable oil
　　1 teaspoon vanilla extract
　　　Vanilla Frosting (recipe follows)
　　　Chocolate stars or blue and red decorating icings (in tube)

To sour milk: Use 1 tablespoon white vinegar plus milk to equal 1 cup.

1. Heat oven to 350°F. Grease and flour muffin cups (2½ inches in diameter) or line with paper bake cups.

2. Combine dry ingredients in large bowl. Add eggs, buttermilk, water, oil and vanilla; beat on medium speed of mixer 2 minutes (batter will be thin). Fill cups ⅔ full with batter.

3. Bake 15 minutes or until wooden pick inserted in centers comes out clean. Remove cupcakes from pan. Cool completely. To make chocolate stars for garnish, if desired, cut several cupcakes into ½-inch slices; cut out star shapes from cake slices. Frost remaining cupcakes. Garnish with chocolate stars or with blue and red decorating icings.

Makes about 30 cupcakes

Vanilla Frosting: Beat ¼ cup (½ stick) softened butter, ¼ cup shortening and 2 teaspoons vanilla extract. Add 1 cup powdered sugar; beat until creamy. Add 3 cups powdered sugar alternately with 3 to 4 tablespoons milk, beating to spreading consistency. Makes about 2⅓ cups frosting.

Firecracker Cake

3 packages (18¼ ounces each) cake mix with pudding in the mix
    (any flavor), plus ingredients to prepare mixes
2 cups strawberry spreadable fruit
3 containers (16 ounces each) vanilla frosting
    Red and blue paste food colorings
    Licorice whip
1 tube (4¼ ounces) white decorator icing with tips

Supplies
3 empty 6-ounce aluminum cans, washed, dried and both
    ends removed

1. Prepare cake mixes according to package directions. Reserve 1 cup batter. Divide remaining batter among 2 (9-inch) greased square baking pans and 4 (7½-inch) greased square disposable baking pans. Generously grease and flour cans. Cover one end of each can tightly with aluminum foil. Pour about ⅓ cup reserved cake batter into each can. Place filled cans on baking sheet.

2. Bake cakes according to package directions. Cool in pans and cans 10 minutes. Remove from pans and cans to wire racks; cool completely. Wrap tightly in plastic wrap; freeze overnight.

3. Trim 2 (7½-inch) cakes to 5-inch squares. Spread one 5-inch cake, one 7½-inch cake and one 9-inch cake with ⅓ cup spreadable fruit each; top each with remaining same-sized cake.

4. Place 1½ containers frosting in medium bowl; tint with red food coloring. Place ½ container frosting in small bowl; tint with blue food coloring. Frost sides of 9-inch cake with red frosting; frost top with white frosting. Frost 1 side of 7½-inch cake with blue frosting; frost remaining sides with white frosting. DO NOT FROST TOP. Frost 1 side of 5-inch cake with blue frosting; frost remaining sides with red frosting and frost top with white frosting. Frost can cakes one each with red, white and blue frosting.

5. Place 9-inch cake on serving platter. Top with 7½-inch cake, turning at an angle to the right. Frost top right corner of 7½-inch cake with blue frosting as shown in photo. Frost the rest of the top of the middle layer white. Add 5-inch cake as top layer, also twisting to the right at the same angle.

continued on page 86

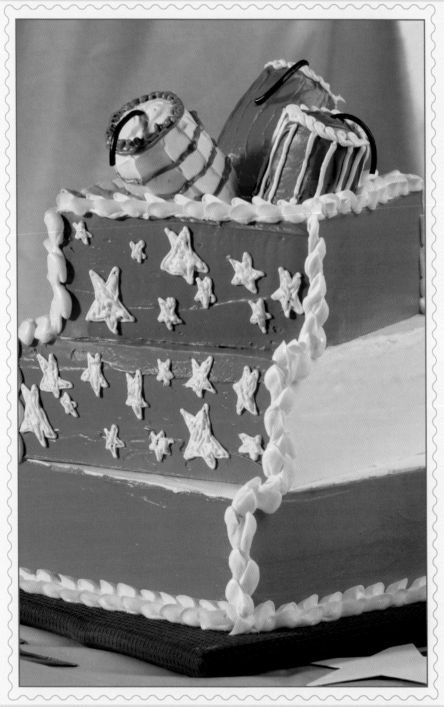

Firecracker Cake, continued

6. Add firecrackers to cake top, cutting ends at angles as necessary. Place remaining frosting in small resealable plastic food storage bags. Cut off tiny corner of each bag; pipe onto firecrackers as desired. Place small piece of licorice in each firecracker for fuse. Pipe border around base and top of cake, and up sides with white decorator icing.

Makes 30 servings

Cherry Oatmeal Bars

¾ cup (1½ sticks) butter or margarine
2 cups firmly packed brown sugar
2 cups all-purpose flour
2 cups old-fashioned or quick-cooking oats, uncooked
2 teaspoons baking soda
1 (21-ounce) can cherry pie filling
2 tablespoons granulated sugar
1 tablespoon cornstarch
½ teaspoon almond extract

Put butter and brown sugar in a large mixing bowl. Beat with an electric mixer on medium speed 3 to 4 minutes, or until well mixed. Combine flour, oats and baking soda. Add flour mixture to sugar mixture; mix on low speed until crumbly.

Spread two-thirds of the oats mixture into the bottom of an ungreased 13×9×2-inch baking pan. Press down to make a firm layer.

Purée cherry pie filling with an electric blender or food processor until smooth. Pour puréed filling into a medium saucepan. Combine granulated sugar and cornstarch; stir into filling. Cook, stirring constantly, over low heat until mixture is thick and bubbly. Stir in almond extract. Pour cherry mixture evenly over oats layer. Crumble remaining oats mixture evenly over cherry layer.

Bake in a preheated 350°F oven 30 to 35 minutes, or until golden brown. Let cool before cutting into bars.   *Makes 32 to 40 bars*

Favorite recipe from **Cherry Marketing Institute**

Jumbo Jack-o'-Lantern Brownie

¾ cup (1½ sticks) butter or margarine, melted
1½ cups sugar
1½ teaspoons vanilla extract
3 eggs
¾ cup all-purpose flour
½ cup HERSHEY'S Cocoa
½ teaspoon baking powder
¼ teaspoon salt
   Orange Buttercream Frosting (recipe follows)
   Decorating icing or gel and assorted candies

1. Heat oven to 350°F. Line 12-inch pizza pan with foil; grease foil.

2. Stir together butter, sugar and vanilla in medium bowl. Add eggs; with spoon, beat well. Stir together flour, cocoa, baking powder and salt; gradually add to egg mixture, stirring until well blended. Spread batter into prepared pan.

3. Bake 20 to 22 minutes or until top springs back when touched lightly in center. Cool completely in pan on wire rack.

4. Remove brownie from pan; peel off foil. Prepare Orange Buttercream Frosting; spread over top of brownie. Garnish as desired with decorating icing and candies to resemble jack-o'-lantern face.

Makes 12 to 15 servings

Orange Buttercream Frosting

3 tablespoons butter or margarine, softened
2 cups powdered sugar
2 tablespoons milk
½ teaspoon vanilla extract
   Red and yellow food colors

Beat butter in small bowl until creamy. Gradually add powdered sugar, milk and vanilla, beating until smooth and of spreading consistency. Add additional milk, 1 teaspoon at a time, if needed. Stir in food colors for desired orange color.

Makes 1 cup frosting

Spider Cupcakes

1 package (18¼ ounces) yellow or white cake mix
1 cup solid-pack pumpkin
¾ cup water
3 eggs
2 tablespoons oil
1 teaspoon ground cinnamon
1 teaspoon pumpkin pie spice*
   Orange food coloring
1 container (16 ounces) vanilla, cream cheese or caramel frosting
⅔ cup (4 ounces) semisweet chocolate
48 black gumdrops

*Substitute ½ teaspoon ground cinnamon, ¼ teaspoon ground ginger and ⅛ teaspoon each ground allspice and ground nutmeg for 1 teaspoon pumpkin pie spice.

1. Preheat oven to 350°F. Line 24 standard (2½-inch) muffin pan cups with paper baking liners, or spray with nonstick cooking spray.

2. Combine cake mix, pumpkin, water, eggs, oil, cinnamon and pumpkin pie spice in bowl. Beat at medium speed of electric mixer 3 minutes or until blended. Spoon ¼ cup batter into each cup. Bake 20 minutes or until toothpicks inserted into centers come out clean. Cool 10 minutes on wire rack. Remove from pan; cool completely.

3. Add orange food coloring to frosting. Stir until well blended; adjust color as needed by adding additional food coloring 1 drop at a time, blending well after each addition. Frost cupcakes.

4. Place chocolate in small resealable plastic food storage bag. Microwave at MEDIUM (50% power) 40 seconds. Knead bag; microwave 30 seconds to 1 minute or until chocolate is melted. Knead bag until chocolate is smooth. Cut tiny corner off one end of bag. Drizzle chocolate in four or five concentric circles over top of cupcake. Immediately draw 6 to 8 lines from center to edges of cupcake with toothpick or knife at regular intervals to make web. Repeat with remaining cupcakes and chocolate.

5. For spider, place one gumdrop in center of web design on top of cupcake. Roll out another gumdrop with rolling pin. Slice thinly and roll into "legs." Place legs onto cupcake to complete spider. Repeat with remaining gumdrops and cupcakes.
Makes 24 cupcakes

Hanukkah Cookies

½ cup (1 stick) unsalted butter, softened
1 package (3 ounces) cream cheese
½ cup sugar
¼ cup honey
1 egg
½ teaspoon vanilla
2½ cups all-purpose flour
⅓ cup finely ground walnuts
1 teaspoon baking powder
¼ teaspoon salt
   Blue, yellow and white icings

1. Beat butter, cream cheese, sugar, honey, egg and vanilla in large bowl at medium speed of electric mixer until creamy. Stir in flour, walnuts, baking powder and salt until well blended. Form dough into ball; wrap in plastic wrap and flatten. Refrigerate about 2 hours or until firm.

2. Preheat oven to 350°F. Lightly grease cookie sheets. Roll out dough, small portion at a time, to ¼-inch thickness on floured surface with lightly floured rolling pin. (Keep remaining dough wrapped in refrigerator.) Cut dough with 2½-inch dreidel-shaped cookie cutter and 6-pointed star cookie cutter. Place 2 inches apart on prepared cookie sheets.

3. Bake 8 to 10 minutes or until edges are lightly browned. Let cookies stand on cookie sheets 1 to 2 minutes; transfer to wire racks to cool completely. Decorate cookies with icings.   *Makes about 40 cookies*

Christmas Wreaths

1 package (18 ounces) refrigerated sugar cookie dough
2 tablespoons all-purpose flour
Green food coloring
Red decorating icing
Green colored sugar or sprinkles

1. Remove dough from wrapper; place in large bowl. Let dough stand at room temperature about 15 minutes.

2. Add flour and green food coloring to dough in bowl; beat at medium speed of electric mixer until dough well blended and evenly colored. Divide dough in half; wrap both halves in plastic wrap and freeze 20 minutes.

3. Preheat oven to 350°F. Grease cookie sheets. For cookie bottoms, roll 1 dough half on lightly floured surface to ⅜-inch thickness. Cut with 3-inch round or fluted cookie cutter; place 2 inches apart on prepared cookie sheets. Using 1-inch round cookie cutter, cut center circle from each cookie.

4. For cookie tops, roll remaining dough half on lightly floured surface to ⅜-inch thickness. Cut with 3-inch round or fluted cookie cutter; place 2 inches apart on prepared cookie sheets. Using 1-inch round cookie cutter, cut center circle from each cookie. Using hors d'oeuvre cutters, miniature cookie cutters or knife, cut tiny circles in half of cutouts. Decorate with green sugar or sprinkles as desired.

5. Bake cutouts 10 minutes or until very lightly browned at edges. Cool on cookie sheet 5 minutes; transfer to wire racks to cool completely.

6. To assemble, spread icing onto flat sides of bottom cookies; place top cookies over icing.   *Makes about 18 sandwich cookies*

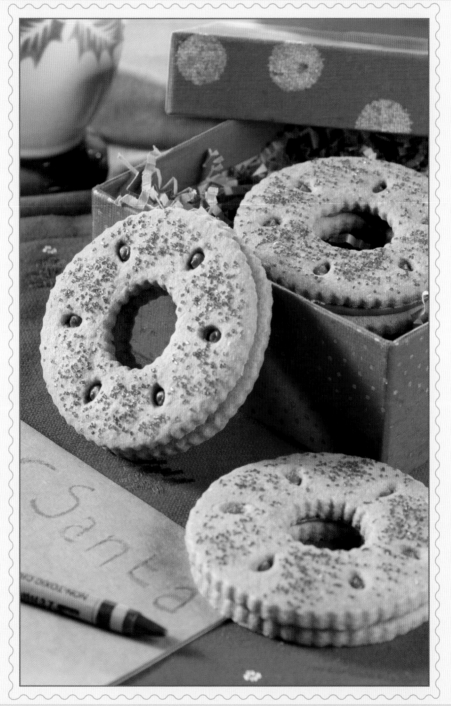

Let it Snow

- **2 (9-inch) round cake layers**
- **2 (10-inch) round cake boards, taped together and covered, or large tray**
- **1½ cups prepared white frosting**
- **½ cup prepared chocolate frosting**
- **Assorted gumdrops**
- **1 sugar ice cream cone, cut in half crosswise**
- **Red pull-apart licorice twists**

1. Cut off small piece from one side of each cake layer to form flat edge (so cake layers will fit together as shown in photo).

2. Using diagram as guide, draw pattern for snowman's head (with hat) on 9-inch circle of waxed paper. Cut out pattern and place on top half of cake. Cut out head. Place head and body of snowman on prepared cake board; attach flat edges of cake layers with small amount of white frosting.

3. Frost hat with chocolate frosting. Frost remaining cake with white frosting.

4. Decorate snowman with assorted gumdrops and ice cream cone nose as shown in photo. Arrange licorice to resemble hatband and scarf as shown in photo. *Makes 16 to 18 servings*

Snowman Head with Hat

Last-Minute Treats

Oh my! You promised to bring classroom treats and just ran out of time.
This chapter saves the day with tasty, easy-to-prepare treats.

Chocolate Cherry Cupcakes

　1 package (about 18 ounces) devil's food cake mix
1⅓ cups water
　3 eggs
½ cup sour cream
⅓ cup oil
　1 cup dried cherries
　1 container (16 ounces) buttercream frosting, divided
25 drops green food coloring
11 maraschino cherries, stems removed and cherries cut in half

1. Preheat oven to 350°F. Line 22 standard (2½-inch) muffin cups with paper baking cups.

2. Beat cake mix, water, eggs, sour cream and oil in large bowl 30 seconds at low speed of electric mixer until just blended. Beat on medium speed 2 minutes or until smooth. Fold in dried cherries.

3. Fill muffin cups ¾ full with batter. Bake 20 to 24 minutes or until wooden pick inserted into centers comes out clean. Cool in pan on wire rack 10 minutes. Remove from pan to wire rack; cool completely.

4. Place ¼ cup frosting in small bowl with food coloring. Stir to combine; set aside.

5. Frost cupcakes with remaining white frosting. Place 1 cherry half, cut-side down, onto each cupcake. Place green frosting in piping bag fitted with writing tip. Pipe a stem and leaf onto each cupcake.

Makes 22 cupcakes

Stuffed Bundles

1 package (10 ounces) refrigerated pizza dough
2 ounces lean ham or turkey ham, chopped
½ cup (2 ounces) shredded reduced-fat sharp Cheddar cheese

1. Preheat oven to 425°F. Coat nonstick 12-cup muffin pan with nonstick cooking spray.

2. Unroll dough on flat surface; cut into 12 pieces, about 4×3 inch rectangles. Divide ham and cheese between dough rectangles. Bring corners of dough together, pinching to seal. Place, smooth side up, in prepared muffin cups.

3. Bake 10 to 12 minutes or until golden. Cool slightly. Pack in covered disposable aluminum pans. Place in insulated bags to keep warm or reheat and serve. *Makes 12 bundles*

Kids' Quesadillas

8 slices American cheese
8 (10-inch) flour tortillas
6 tablespoons *French's*® Sweet & Tangy Honey Mustard
½ pound thinly sliced deli turkey
2 tablespoons melted butter
¼ teaspoon paprika

1. To prepare 1 quesadilla, arrange 2 slices of cheese on 1 tortilla. Top with one-fourth of the turkey. Spread with *1½ tablespoons* mustard, then top with another tortilla. Prepare 3 more quesadillas with remaining ingredients.

2. Combine butter and paprika. Brush one side of tortilla with butter mixture. Preheat 12-inch nonstick skillet over medium-high heat. Arrange tortilla butter side down and cook 2 minutes. Brush tortilla with butter mixture and turn over. Cook 1½ minutes or until golden brown. Repeat with remaining three quesadillas. Slice into wedges before serving. *Makes 4 servings*

Note: Carry quesadillas to school in covered disposable aluminum pans. Pack in insulated bags to keep warm.

Rock 'n' Rollers

8 (6- to 7-inch) flour tortillas
1 package (8 ounces) Neufchâtel cheese, softened
⅔ cup peach preserves
2 cups (8 ounces) shredded fat-free Cheddar cheese
1 cup packed washed fresh spinach leaves
6 ounces thinly sliced regular or smoked turkey breast

1. Spread each tortilla evenly with 1 ounce Neufchâtel cheese; cover with thin layer of preserves. Sprinkle with Cheddar cheese.

2. Arrange spinach leaves and turkey over Cheddar cheese. Roll up tortillas; trim ends. Place rollers in covered plastic container. Refrigerate until ready to serve.

3. Pack containers in insulated bags with frozen ice packs. To serve, cut each roller crosswise in half or diagonally into 1-inch pieces.

Makes 16 to 24 roll-up slices

Sassy Salsa Rollers: Substitute salsa for peach preserves and shredded iceberg lettuce for spinach leaves.

Ham 'n' Apple Rollers: Omit peach preserves and spinach leaves. Substitute lean ham slices for turkey. Spread tortillas with Neufchâtel cheese as directed; sprinkle with Cheddar cheese. Top each tortilla with about 2 tablespoons finely chopped apple and 2 ham slices; roll up. Continue as directed.

Play It Safe

Keep hot food hot and cold food cold: 140°F or above for hot food, 40° F or below for cold food. To keep food cool, use an insulated bag with a frozen ice pack. Carry hot food in a thermos or insulated bag.

Pizza Rollers

2 packages (10 ounces each) refrigerated pizza dough
1 cup pizza sauce
36 slices turkey pepperoni
12 sticks mozzarella cheese

1. Preheat oven to 425°F. Coat baking sheet with nonstick cooking spray.

2. Roll out pizza dough on baking sheet to form 12×9-inch rectangle. Cut pizza dough into 6 (4½×4-inch) rectangles. Repeat with remaining dough. Spread about 1 tablespoon sauce over center third of each rectangle. Top with 3 slices pepperoni and stick of mozzarella cheese. Bring ends of dough together over cheese, pinching to seal. Place seam side down on prepared baking sheet.

3. Bake in center of oven 10 minutes or until golden brown. Cool slightly. Place warm Pizza Rollers in disposable aluminum pans. Pack in insulated bags to carry to school. Either serve immediately or reheat at school.

Makes 12 rollers

Tasty Teaching Time

Sandwiches and snacks are a lot more likely to be eaten if they are served in small sizes. Small portions not only avoid wasting food but encourage students to taste unfamiliar foods that may be less appealing in large servings.

Dizzy Dogs

2 packages (8 breadsticks or 11 ounces each) refrigerated
   breadsticks
2 packages (16 ounces each) hot dogs (16 hot dogs)
2 egg whites
   Sesame and/or poppy seeds
   Mustard, ketchup and barbecue sauce (optional)

1. Preheat oven to 375°F.

2. Using 1 breadstick for each, wrap hot dogs with dough in spiral
pattern. Brush breadstick dough with egg white and sprinkle with
sesame and/or poppy seeds. Place on ungreased baking sheet.

3. Bake 12 to 15 minutes or until light golden brown. Cool slightly.
Place in covered disposable aluminum pans. Carry to school in
insulated bags. Serve immediately or reheat and serve with
condiments for dipping, if desired.   *Makes 16 hot dogs*

Taco Cups

1 pound lean ground beef, turkey or pork
1 package (1 ounce) LAWRY'S® Taco Spices & Seasonings
1¼ cups water
¼ cup salsa
2 packages (8 ounces each) refrigerator biscuits
½ cup (2 ounces) shredded cheddar cheese

In medium skillet, brown ground beef until crumbly; drain fat. Stir in
Taco Spices & Seasonings and water. Bring to a boil; reduce heat to low
and cook, uncovered, 10 minutes. Stir in salsa. Separate biscuits and
press each biscuit into an ungreased muffin cup. Spoon equal amounts
of meat mixture into each muffin cup; sprinkle each with cheese. Bake,
uncovered, in 350°F oven for 12 minutes.

Makes about 16 taco cups

Note: Cool cups slightly in pans. Cover and pack muffin pans in
insulated bags to carry to school. Serve immediately or reheat in pans.

Rainbow Spirals

4 (10-inch) flour tortillas (assorted flavors and colors)
4 tablespoons *French's*® Mustard (any flavor)
½ pound (about 8 slices) thinly sliced deli roast beef, bologna or turkey
8 slices American, provolone or Muenster cheese
Fancy Party Toothpicks

1. Spread each tortilla with *1 tablespoon* mustard. Layer with meat and cheeses, dividing evenly.

2. Roll up jelly-roll style; secure with toothpicks and cut into thirds. Arrange on platter.   *Makes 12 roll-up slices*

Prep Time: 10 minutes

Note: For classroom treats, eliminate the toothpicks. Wrap each roll securely in plastic wrap. Refrigerate before cutting to serve.

Monster Finger Sandwiches

2 cans (11 ounces) refrigerated breadstick dough (12 breadsticks)
Mustard
24 slices deli ham, cut into ½-inch strips
8 slices Monterey Jack cheese, cut into ½-inch strips
2 egg yolks, lightly beaten
Assorted food colorings

1. Preheat oven to 350°F. Place 6 breadsticks on ungreased baking sheets. Spread with mustard as desired. Divide ham strips evenly among breadsticks, placing over mustard. Repeat with cheese. Top with remaining 6 breadsticks. Gently stretch top dough over filling; press dough together to seal.

2. Score knuckle and nail lines into each sandwich using sharp knife. Do not cut completely through dough. Tint egg yolk with food coloring as desired. Paint nail with egg yolk mixture.

3. Bake on lower oven rack 12 to 13 minutes or just until golden. Let cool slightly. Serve warm or cool completely.   *Makes 12 servings*

Conversation Heart Cereal Treats

20 large marshmallows
2 tablespoons margarine or butter
3 cups frosted oat cereal with marshmallow bits
16 large conversation hearts

1. Line 8- or 9-inch square pan with aluminum foil, leaving 2-inch overhangs on 2 sides. Generously grease or spray with nonstick cooking spray.

2. Melt marshmallows and margarine in medium saucepan over medium heat 3 minutes or until melted and smooth, stirring constantly. Remove from heat.

3. Add cereal; stir until completely coated. Spread in prepared pan; press evenly onto bottom using greased rubber spatula. Press heart candies into top of treats while still warm, evenly spacing to allow 1 heart per bar. Let cool 10 minutes. Using foil overhangs as handles, remove treats from pan. Cut into 16 bars. *Makes 16 bars*

Prep and Cook Time: 18 minutes

Make It Special

Select novelty candles in shapes of numerals, cartoon figures, and also novelty candle holders to quickly decorate a cakes and cupcakes.

Hershey's Easy Chocolate Cracker Snacks

1⅔ cups (10-ounce package) HERSHEY'S Mint Chocolate Chips*

2 cups (12-ounce package) HERSHEY'S Semi-Sweet Chocolate Chips

2 tablespoons shortening (do not use butter, margarine, spread or oil)

60 to 70 round buttery crackers (about one-half 1-pound box)

2 cups (11.5-ounce package) HERSHEY'S Milk Chocolate Chips and ¼ teaspoon pure peppermint extract can be substituted for mint chocolate chips.

1. Line several trays or cookie sheets with waxed paper.

2. Place mint chocolate chips, chocolate chips and shortening in large microwave-safe bowl. Microwave at HIGH (100%) 1 minute; stir. Continue heating 30 seconds at a time, stirring after each heating, until chips are melted and mixture is smooth when stirred.

3. Drop crackers into chocolate mixture one at a time. Using tongs, push cracker into chocolate so that it is covered completely. (If chocolate begins to thicken, reheat 10 to 20 seconds in microwave.) Remove from chocolate, tapping lightly on edge of bowl to remove excess chocolate. Place on prepared tray. Refrigerate until chocolate hardens, about 20 minutes. For best results, store tightly covered in refrigerator.   *Makes about 66 snacks*

Peanut Butter and Milk Chocolate: Use 1⅔ cups (10-ounce package) REESE'S® Peanut Butter Chips, 2 cups (11.5-ounce package) HERSHEY'S Milk Chocolate Chips and 2 tablespoons shortening. Proceed as above.

Chocolate Raspberry: Use 1⅔ cups (10-ounce package) HERSHEY'S Raspberry Chips, 2 cups (11.5-ounce package) HERSHEY'S Milk Chocolate Chips and 2 tablespoons shortening. Proceed as above.

White Chip and Toffee: Melt 1⅔ cups (10-ounce package) HERSHEY'S Premier White Chips and 1 tablespoon shortening. Dip Crackers; before coating hardens sprinkle with SKOR® English Toffee Bits or HEATH® BITS 'O BRICKLE® Almond Toffee Bits.

Ice Cream Cone Cupcakes

    1 package (18¼ ounces) white cake mix
        plus ingredients to prepare mix
    2 tablespoons nonpareils*
   24 flat-bottomed ice cream cones
      Vanilla and chocolate frosting
      Candies and other decorations

*Nonpareils are tiny, round, brightly colored sprinkles used for cake and cookie decorating.

Preheat oven to 350°F. Prepare cake mix according to package directions. Stir in nonpareils. Spoon ¼ cup batter into each ice cream cone. Stand cones in 13×9-inch baking pan or muffin tins. Bake cones until toothpick inserted into centers of cakes comes out clean, about 20 minutes. Cool on wire racks. Frost each filled cone. Decorate as desired.   *Makes 24 cupcakes*

Note: Cupcakes are best served the day they are prepared. Store loosely covered.

Glazed Donut Cookies

    2 packages (18 ounces each) refrigerated oatmeal raisin
        cookie dough in squares or rounds (12 count)
      Prepared white or chocolate frosting
      Assorted white or chocolate frosting

Preheat oven to 350°F. Grease 24 standard (2½-inch) muffin pan cups. Remove dough from wrapper. Separate dough into 12 pieces; let stand at room temperature about 15 minutes. Shape each dough piece into 12-inch-long rope on lightly floured surface. Coil ropes into muffin cups, leaving centers open. Bake 12 minutes; remove from oven and re-shape center hole with round handle of wooden spoon. Return to oven; bake 3 to 4 minutes or until set. Remove from oven; reshape holes, if necessary. Cool in pan 4 minutes; transfer cookies to wire racks to cool completely. Spread frosting over cookies; decorate with sprinkles.   *Makes 24 cookies*

Brownie Gems

1 package DUNCAN HINES® Chocolate Lover's® Double
    Fudge Brownie Mix
2 eggs
2 tablespoons water
⅓ cup vegetable oil
28 miniature peanut butter cup or chocolate kiss candies
1 container of your favorite Duncan Hines frosting

1. Preheat oven to 350°F. Spray (1¾-inch) mini-muffin pans with vegetable cooking spray or line with foil baking cups.

2. Combine brownie mix, fudge packet from mix, eggs, water and oil in large bowl. Stir with spoon until well blended, about 50 strokes. Drop 1 heaping teaspoonful of batter into each muffin cup; top with candy. Cover candy with more batter. Bake at 350°F for 15 to 17 minutes.

3. Cool 5 minutes. Carefully loosen brownies from pan. Remove to wire racks to cool completely. Frost and decorate as desired.

Makes 28 brownie gems

Number One Cake

1 (13×9-inch) cake
1 (19×13-inch) cake board, cut in half crosswise and covered
1½ cups prepared white frosting
    Yellow food coloring
    Assorted colored candies

1. Trim top and sides of cake. Draw a number 1 pattern on 13×9-inch piece of waxed paper. Cut pattern out and place on cake. Cut out cake around the pattern; place on prepared cake board. Reserve extra cake for another use.

2. Tint frosting yellow; frost cake. Decorate with assorted candies as desired.

Makes 16 servings

Sugar-and-Spice Twists

  1 tablespoon sugar
  ¼ teaspoon ground cinnamon
  1 package (6-count) refrigerated breadsticks

1. Preheat oven to 350°F. Spray baking sheet with nonstick cooking spray; set aside.

2. Combine sugar and cinnamon in shallow dish or plate; set aside.

3. Divide breadstick dough into 6 pieces. Roll each piece into 12-inch rope. Roll in sugar-cinnamon mixture. Twist into pretzel shape. Place on prepared baking sheet. Bake 15 to 18 minutes or until lightly browned. Remove from baking sheet. Cool 5 minutes. Serve warm.

Makes 6 servings

Hint: Use colored sugar sprinkles in place of the sugar in this recipe for a fun 'twist' of color that's perfect for holidays, birthdays or simple everyday celebrations.

Quick & Easy Pumpkin Cupcakes

  1 package (18.25 ounces) spice cake mix
  1 can (15 ounces) LIBBY'S® 100% Pure Pumpkin
  3 large eggs
  ⅓ cup vegetable oil
  ⅓ cup water
  1 container (16 ounces) prepared cream cheese or vanilla frosting
    Assorted sprinkles

PREHEAT oven to 350°F. Paper-line or grease 24 muffin cups.

BLEND cake mix, pumpkin, eggs, vegetable oil and water in large mixer bowl until moistened. Beat on medium speed for 2 minutes. Pour batter into prepared muffin cups, filling ¾ full.

BAKE for 18 to 23 minutes or until wooden pick inserted in centers comes out clean. Cool in pan on wire rack for 10 minutes; remove to wire racks to cool completely. Spread cupcakes with frosting. Decorate as desired.

Makes 24 cupcakes

Kids' Wrap

  5 tablespoons Dijon honey mustard
  8 (8-inch) fat-free flour tortillas
  8 slices reduced-fat American cheese, cut in half
  1 pound thinly sliced fat-free oven-roasted turkey breast
  1 cup shredded carrot (about 1 medium)
 12 romaine or leafy green lettuce leaves, washed and torn
    into bite-size pieces

1. Spread about 2 teaspoons mustard evenly over one tortilla.

2. Top with 2 cheese halves, half of turkey, half of shredded carrots and half of torn lettuce.

3. Roll up tortilla and cut in half. Repeat with remaining ingredients. Wrap tortillas individually in plastic wrap or place in covered plastic container. Refrigerate. Carry to school in insulated bags with frozen ice packs.   *Makes 16 pieces*

Tasty Teaching Time

Food wrapped in edible bundles always tastes twice as delightful. Flour tortilla wraps like Kids' Wrap are a child-friendly way to contribute toward the recommended servings of fruits and vegetables for a day.

Cinnamon-Raisin Roll-Ups

     1 package (8 ounces) reduced-fat cream cheese, softened
     1 cup shredded carrots
     ½ cup golden or regular raisins
     2 tablespoons honey
     ½ teaspoon ground cinnamon
     8 (7- to 8-inch) whole wheat or regular flour tortillas
    16 thin apple wedges (optional)

1. Combine cream cheese, carrot, raisins, honey and cinnamon in small bowl; mix well.

2. Spread tortillas evenly with cream cheese mixture, leaving ½-inch border around edge of each tortilla. Place 2 apple wedges down center of each tortilla, if desired; roll up. Wrap in plastic wrap. Refrigerate until ready to serve. *Makes 8 roll-ups*

Save Time

For extra convenience, prepare roll-ups the night before. Pack in covered plastic containers and refrigerate. At the same time put small juice boxes in the freezer. In the morning, pack roll-ups along with frozen juice boxes in coolers. The juice boxes will thaw by serving time and will keep the snacks cold in the meantime.

The publisher would like to thank the companies and organizations listed below for the use of their recipes and photographs in this publication.

Cherry Marketing Institute

Duncan Hines® and Moist Deluxe® are registered trademarks of Aurora Foods Inc.

Hershey Foods Corporation

The Hidden Valley® Food Products Company

JOLLY TIME® Pop Corn

Keebler® Company

Lawry's® Foods

® Mars, Incorporated 2004

National Honey Board

Nestlé USA

Reckitt Benckiser Inc.

The Sugar Association, Inc.

METRIC CONVERSION CHART

VOLUME MEASUREMENTS (dry)

1/8 teaspoon = 0.5 mL
1/4 teaspoon = 1 mL
1/2 teaspoon = 2 mL
3/4 teaspoon = 4 mL
1 teaspoon = 5 mL
1 tablespoon = 15 mL
2 tablespoons = 30 mL
1/4 cup = 60 mL
1/3 cup = 75 mL
1/2 cup = 125 mL
2/3 cup = 150 mL
3/4 cup = 175 mL
1 cup = 250 mL
2 cups = 1 pint = 500 mL
3 cups = 750 mL
4 cups = 1 quart = 1 L

VOLUME MEASUREMENTS (fluid)

1 fluid ounce (2 tablespoons) = 30 mL
4 fluid ounces (1/2 cup) = 125 mL
8 fluid ounces (1 cup) = 250 mL
12 fluid ounces (1 1/2 cups) = 375 mL
16 fluid ounces (2 cups) = 500 mL

WEIGHTS (mass)

1/2 ounce = 15 g
1 ounce = 30 g
3 ounces = 90 g
4 ounces = 120 g
8 ounces = 225 g
10 ounces = 285 g
12 ounces = 360 g
16 ounces = 1 pound = 450 g

DIMENSIONS

1/16 inch = 2 mm
1/8 inch = 3 mm
1/4 inch = 6 mm
1/2 inch = 1.5 cm
3/4 inch = 2 cm
1 inch = 2.5 cm

OVEN TEMPERATURES

250°F = 120°C
275°F = 140°C
300°F = 150°C
325°F = 160°C
350°F = 180°C
375°F = 190°C
400°F = 200°C
425°F = 220°C
450°F = 230°C

BAKING PAN SIZES

Utensil	Size in Inches/Quarts	Metric Volume	Size in Centimeters
Baking or Cake Pan (square or rectangular)	8×8×2	2 L	20×20×5
	9×9×2	2.5 L	23×23×5
	12×8×2	3 L	30×20×5
	13×9×2	3.5 L	33×23×5
Loaf Pan	8×4×3	1.5 L	20×10×7
	9×5×3	2 L	23×13×7
Round Layer Cake Pan	8×1½	1.2 L	20×4
	9×1½	1.5 L	23×4
Pie Plate	8×1¼	750 mL	20×3
	9×1¼	1 L	23×3
Baking Dish or Casserole	1 quart	1 L	—
	1½ quart	1.5 L	—
	2 quart	2 L	—